# INTERNET INVENTORS

BY NEL YOMTOV

**CHILDREN'S PRESS**®

# BRINGING HISTORY to LIFE

Content Consultant
James Marten, PhD
Professor and Chair, History Department
Marquette University
Milwaukee, Wisconsin

Library of Congress Cataloging-in-Publication Data

Yomtov, Nelson.
   Internet inventors / by Nel Yomtov.
      p. cm. — (Cornerstones of freedom)
   Includes bibliographical references and index.
   ISBN 978-0-531-23609-3 (library binding) — ISBN 978-0-531-21967-6 (pbk.)
1. Internet—History—Juvenile literature. 2. Inventors—Biography—
Juvenile literature. I. Title. II. Series: Cornerstones of freedom.

TK5105.875.I57Y64 2013
004.67'80922—dc23                              2012034323

All rights reserved. Published in 2013 by Children's Press, an imprint of
Scholastic Inc.
Printed in the United States of America 113

SCHOLASTIC, CHILDREN'S PRESS, CORNERSTONES OF FREEDOM™,
and associated logos are trademarks and/or registered trademarks of
Scholastic Inc.

1 2 3 4 5 6 7 8 9 10 R 22 21 20 19 18 17 16 15 14 13

Photographs © 2013: Alamy Images: 30 (Andre Jenny), 27 (M. Berman/
ClassicStock), 5 top, 40 (M4OS Photos), 5 bottom, 35 (Richard Levine);
AP Images: 50 (Bob Jordan), 25, 57 top (fls), 45 (Kyodo), 33 (Marty
Lederhandler), 14, 56 (Reed Saxon), 38 (Richard Drew), 48 (The Canadian
Press, Ross D. Franklin), 4 top, 55 (The Gleaner, Mike Lawrence), 8, 32;
Computer History Museum/Mark Richards: 10; Getty Images: 51 (Reza
Estakhrian), 24 (Science & Society Picture Library); iStockphoto/johan63:
cover; Landov: 16 (Felix Ordonez/Reuters), 26 (Roger L. Wollenberg/UPI);
Library of Congress/Fabian Bachrach: 12; Louis Fabian Bachrach: 17;
Photo Researchers: 42 (David R. Frazier Photolibrary, Inc.), 6 (Richard
Hutchings); Courtesy of Raytheon BBN Technologies: 15, 21; Reuters/Fred
Prouser: 18; Shutterstock, Inc.: 39 (Annette Shaff), 20 (Jerry Horbert), 54
(Luis Louro), back cover (Toria), 7 (wavebreakmedia); SuperStock, Inc.: 47
(age fotostock), 2, 3, 28 (ClassicStock.com), 31 (Marka), 22 (Photri Images),
11 (Science and Society); The Image Works: 36 (CERN/SSPL), 4 bottom, 49,
57 bottom (Jack Kurtz), 44, 59 (John Birdsall), 23 (Science Museum/SSPL).

Maps by XNR Productions, Inc.

# Did you know that studying history can be fun?

**BRING HISTORY TO LIFE** by becoming a history investigator. Examine the evidence (primary and secondary source materials); cross-examine the people and witnesses. Take a look at what was happening at the time—but be careful! What happened years ago might suddenly become incredibly interesting and change the way you think!

# Contents

# World with a Web

**Many people today rely on the Web to keep in touch with family and friends.**

The World Wide Web is everywhere. It is a giant electronic highway crisscrossing our planet. Today, just about anyone with a computer or a smartphone can be a traveler on this amazing global **network**. It's hard to imagine life without the Web. With just the flick of a finger or the push of a button, we can use the Web to communicate, gather information, shop, play games, and much more.

## CHINA HAS MORE INTERNET

The **Internet**—the larger network that the Web is a part of—is important to almost everyone today. Its origins date back to the late 1950s, when there were no personal computers like the ones we use now. The Internet is the result of decades of research and new ideas. It was built by many people over a long period of time.

Who are these people who changed the way we interact with our world? The creators of the Internet may not be as well known as popular athletes or celebrities. But their work grew the Internet from a single, small network in the United States to an amazing phenomenon linking billions of devices around the world. These individuals changed our world in ways that could not have been imagined even just a few years ago. Let's take a look behind the scenes at some of the movers and shakers who shaped the birth and growth of the World Wide Web.

**Thanks to smartphones and tablet computers, people can access the Internet from almost anywhere.**

**USERS THAN ANY OTHER NATION.**

# CHAPTER I

# THE CREATORS OF THE ARPANET

Early computers were too large and complicated for people to use in their homes.

IN THE 1950S, MOST COMPUTER systems were very large, often filling an entire room. They were called mainframe computers. Mainframes were expensive to build and operate. These huge computers were located mainly at universities, corporations, and government offices. They were used for such tasks as performing mathematical functions and encoding secret messages.

**Transferring information over a modem was very similar to making a phone call from one computer to another.**

Computer operators used **modems** to exchange data over telephone lines. Information could be sent back and forth between computers, but they weren't fully networked. In other words, the information in one system was not available for other systems to browse. Yet there was little urgency about developing such an interconnected network. That changed in 1957, with the announcement of some earthshaking news.

## Sputnik I Stuns the United States

The headline "Soviet Fires Earth Satellite Into Space . . . Sphere Tracked in 4 Crossings Over U.S." streamed across the front page of the *New York Times* on October 5, 1957. Americans were stunned by the surprising news of the world's first successful space launch and orbit. The Soviet Union—not the United States—was the world's leader in technology.

Following World War II (1939–1945), the United States and the Union of Soviet Socialist Republics (USSR) had been engaged in a tense rivalry called the Cold War. Each country jostled for military, scientific, and technological superiority. The race to be the first into space was a huge part of the rivalry.

With *Sputnik*'s successful launch, U.S. government officials feared that the USSR might have other capabilities that could threaten the security of the United States. Could the Soviets launch a nuclear attack against the United States? Could the Soviets interfere with U.S. military communications if there was a war? No one knew the answers.

**The launch of *Sputnik 1* helped fuel the rivalry between the United States and the Soviet Union.**

Suddenly, the U.S. government recognized the need for an electronic communication network that couldn't be knocked out by the Soviets. In 1958, President Dwight D. Eisenhower commissioned the Department of Defense to create the Advanced Research Projects Agency (ARPA) to meet the challenge. ARPA's mission was "to prevent technological surprise from this nation's adversaries and to assure that the United States maintains a lead in applying state-of-the-art technology to military capabilities."

President Dwight Eisenhower authorized the Advanced Research Projects Agency to help defeat the Soviets in the race for new technology.

## Putting the Pieces in Place

In 1962, Dr. J. C. R. Licklider of the Massachusetts Institute of Technology (MIT) was brought on as head of the Information Processing Techniques Office (IPTO), the division that funded ARPA. In 1960, Licklider had published a paper that described his vision of people linked by computers around the world, interacting and sharing information. He called his idea the Galactic Network.

During his two years as ARPA's leader, Licklider assembled a team of computer scientists to help create the network. He convinced Leonard Kleinrock, a professor at the University of California, Los Angeles (UCLA), to join him. In 1961, Kleinrock had written about a way of electronically transmitting data in small blocks called packets. Packet switching, as it came to be known, remains the basis of computer networking today.

In 1966, MIT researcher Lawrence Roberts joined ARPA to refine the concept of packet switching and help develop the network. With assistance from non-ARPA researchers Wesley Clark at Washington University in St. Louis, Paul Baran at the RAND Corporation, and Donald

## Packet Switching

Leonard Kleinrock (above) was the brain behind packet switching, in which a computer divides a computer file into smaller blocks called packets. The packets are transmitted to their destination along different electronic paths at the same time. Once all of the packets arrive, they are reassembled into a single file for the computer user to view. Because many small pieces are able to travel at once, packet switching is faster and more efficient than sending one huge file. If one of the packets gets closed out of a pathway, it uses another path while the other packets continue on their journey to the user's computer.

Davies at England's National Physical Laboratory, the team designed a system that was finally ready to be put to the test.

On October 29, 1969, a computer at UCLA was linked by telephone line to another computer at the Stanford Research Institute (SRI) in Menlo Park, California. The researchers at UCLA typed the letter L on their computer keyboard. Miles away, the letter appeared on the computer screen in Menlo Park. Another letter was typed, and it too was received.

Then suddenly, the system crashed!

Despite the crash, the test was a success. The ARPA team had found a way for computers to talk to each other. After seven years of inventing, engineering, and building, ARPA had created the first computer network. It was appropriately named ARPANET.

## ARPANET Takes Off

Many of the ARPA researchers were scientists and educators at universities in the United States. In ARPA's early stages, four universities—UCLA, the Stanford Research Institute, the University of Utah, and the University of California at Santa Barbara—were the first sites to have large "host" computers hooked into the ARPANET.

Fifteen sites were connected by the end of 1971, and more were joining the network regularly. Some sites were run by the U.S. Air Force, which had happily reported that the network was "twelve times faster and cheaper" than other forms of message transmission they were using. Scientists and researchers around the country began using the network to share useful information with one another.

The technology company Bolt, Beranek, and Newman hosted one of the first ARPANET computers.

## Ray Tomlinson's @ Symbol

By mid-1971, electronic mail, or e-mail, was already known to most ARPANET users. Simple programs allowed users to transfer messages from one computer to another. The message was placed in an electronic mailbox file. The file could not be changed or forwarded, and only people with accounts on the same computer could exchange mail.

Computer programmer Ray Tomlinson had a solution to this problem. He redesigned existing programs to allow mail to be sent back and forth between computers across the network. He also made it possible for the network to accept a new form of e-mail address. These

**Ray Tomlinson changed the Internet forever with his invention of the modern e-mail address.**

addresses included the name of the computer that hosted the mail recipient's account.

Tomlinson's solution was to add the now familiar "@" symbol to all e-mail addresses. The "@" indicated that the user was "at" some other host. The address looked like this: user-account-name@host-computer-name.

Tomlinson's groundbreaking work caught on with university students, researchers, and everyone with access to the ARPANET. E-mail poured across the network like never before. Suddenly, the ARPANET was transformed from a network of computers into a network of people.

## SPOTLIGHT ON

### Wesley Clark

Each of the four large computers in ARPANET's early network used different programs and worked differently. Wesley Clark, a computer researcher at Washington University in St. Louis, had the solution to overcome this communication barrier. Clark convinced Lawrence Roberts that each main computer should be attached to a minicomputer. The minicomputer would serve as the host computer's connection to the network. The smaller computers would be designed to use the same programs and speak the same language. They would handle the packet-switching operations and ease the demands on the host computers and the people running them. This network of minicomputers was called the subnet.

# CHAPTER 2

# MOVERS AND SHAKERS

Lawrence Roberts (left) recognized that DARPANET could be useful for people around the world.

IN THE EARLY 1970S, ACCESS to the ARPANET was limited mainly to the military, universities, and large corporations. By this time, ARPA's name had been changed to DARPA. The *D* was added to represent "Defense." At the same time, ARPANET was renamed DARPANET. Lawrence Roberts, who was running IPTO at the time, realized that the network had far outgrown its original purpose of being a tool for military research and development. Roberts wanted to make access to the DARPANET available to a larger audience.

Roberts believed that packet switching was the way to meet the growing demand for computer communications and networking. All he had to do was find a company that was willing to take over the development of the technology and make it available to the public.

## Telenet Opens the Information Superhighway

Roberts targeted communications giant AT&T as the ideal company to meet the challenge. He approached AT&T about taking over the DARPANET and the development

Roberts believed that AT&T's experience with massive telephone networks would make it a perfect candidate for expanding the DARPANET.

**From left to right, Richard Bolt, Robert Newman, and Leo Beranek founded their technology company in 1948.**

of packet-switching technology. AT&T turned down his offer, but Roberts was determined to get networking technology to the public as soon as possible.

He then approached the Bolt, Beranek and Newman Corporation (BBN). BBN had helped build the ARPANET. Roberts proposed a clever idea to the company. He thought BBN might be interested in setting up a packet-

# YESTERDAY'S HEADLINES

Since the birth of computer technology, some Americans have believed that the government uses computers to keep secret files on U.S. citizens. On June 24, 1975, the *New York Times* reported that David O. Cooke, a deputy assistant secretary at the Department of Defense (above), denied such claims. Referring to the Pentagon's use of the ARPANET, Cooke said, "Let me emphasize that it is not a 'secret network,' that it is used for scientific research purposes, that it contains no sociological or intelligence data on personalities, and that it is a marvel in many ways."

switching network as a government-regulated communications company. BBN was hesitant at first but eventually agreed to the suggestion. By 1975, it had founded a company called Telenet. Telenet operated the world's first commercial packet-switching network. Roberts had left IPTO in 1973 to become the head of Telenet.

In addition to providing network access through telephone lines, Telenet also manufactured the **hardware** used to build networks. Companies began setting up their own networks using Telenet's products. Giant corporations such as General Motors and Southern Bell became part of the blossoming information superhighway.

## Valuable Experimentation

Around the time Roberts left DARPA, Robert Kahn joined the organization as a program manager. Kahn had been a researcher at BBN. He was interested in applying packet-switching technology to land-based radio and satellite radio as a means to transmit data. Land-based radio, which relies on antennas to transmit messages between users, was a sensible choice because radio equipment could be moved from place to place during battles. Packet-switching satellite radio would be able to provide global communications and monitor military operations.

Under Kahn's guidance, DARPA built a packet-switching radio network in the San Francisco Bay area. The system was called PRNET (PR for packet radio). It included a control station, **broadcasting** equipment, and radio sets that could be hooked up to computers. The system was intended to make voice transmission more efficient. Furthermore, enemies would have difficulty listening in on a conversation

**Robert Kahn used packet switching to transmit information between computers over the air.**

**Communications satellites allowed people to transfer information around the world without the use of wired networks.**

because the voice message would be **digitized** and broken into packets. PRNET was never used in combat, but its technology would soon be used for a greater purpose.

In 1975, Kahn created the Atlantic Packet Satellite Network (SATNET). SATNET was a packet-switching satellite radio system. It was developed with assistance from the British Post Office and the Norwegian Telecommunications Authority. The packet-switching system linked four sites: one in West Virginia, one in

## AN ACCURATE PREDICTION

In 1982, the National Science Foundation issued a study that claimed that electronic information technology would transform all aspects of life in America by the year 2000. In an article published on June 14, 1982, the *New York Times* reported the study's claim that the technology's effect on society would be as deeply felt as those of the automobile and television. See page 60 for a link to view the article.

Maryland, one in Norway, and one in England. SATNET was one of networking's first international cooperative efforts. It would not be the last.

## Creating the Internet

Kahn and his associates at DARPA were now operating three separate networks: ARPANET, PRNET, and SATNET. Each network used packet switching but in a slightly different way. Therefore, the three networks were unable to communicate with one another. Kahn began to work on bringing them together.

**Robert Kahn sought the help of Vinton Cerf (right) in connecting ARPANET, PRNET, and SATNET.**

He teamed up with Stanford University professor Vinton Cerf to develop a system for internetworking, or connecting networks together. The pair was assisted by other DARPA team members and a variety of researchers who were planning their own packet-switching networks. Following many months of discussion, the participants agreed to adapt the same **protocol** for all of their networks. They called it Transmission Control Protocol (TCP). It took several years to develop the protocol and put it into practice.

Eventually, test sites were ready to try out DARPA's first multinetwork connection. In a demonstration conducted in July 1977, packets of data were successfully sent from California through PRNET, then through the DARPANET

For their efforts in helping to create the Internet, Cerf (left) and Kahn (center) were awarded the Presidential Medal of Freedom in 2005 by President George W. Bush (right).

via SATNET on the East Coast, over SATNET to Europe, and then back through DARPANET to California.

By demonstrating that TCP could connect different networks, the experiment signaled the birth of the Internet. TCP was later refined to make the system more efficient, resulting in a protocol called TCP/IP (IP for internet protocol). A computer on any network could use TCP/IP to communicate with a computer on any other network. Kahn, Cerf, and their associates had created the Internet, a system with potentially unlimited room for growth.

## TODAY'S PERSPECTIVE

The DARPANET no longer exists today. Even before it was officially closed down, this Internet pioneer experienced major changes. In 1983, DARPANET was split into two separate networks: DARPANET and MILNET (MIL for military). The DARPANET continued as a civilian research network. MILNET was dedicated strictly to Department of Defense traffic. In 1987, the National Science Foundation took over the responsibility of running the DARPANET from DARPA. DARPANET was officially shut down in February 1990. In about 20 years, it had grown from four original university hosts to more than 300,000 hosts worldwide.

# CHAPTER 3

# ON THE WAY TO THE WEB

Home computers became more and more common throughout the 1980s.

EVEN BY THE LATE 1970s, only a few thousand people had access to the Internet. These were mostly university professors, military and government personnel, and students.

The early pioneers of the ARPANET and the Internet, however, had set the stage for an online explosion that no one could have imagined in earlier years. In the late 1970s and early 1980s, companies began manufacturing personal computers and modems for home use. During this time, innovative thinkers created new networks and other online services that changed the face of global communications.

**The earliest version of USENET connected the University of North Carolina (above) with Duke University.**

## USENET

University students were particularly eager to tap into the new Internet technology. In 1979, two Duke University students named Steve Bellovin and Tom Truscott set up a news exchange system between Duke and the University of North Carolina. They called it USENET. It used dial-up telephone connections and operated independently of DARPANET. Soon, students at other universities joined the new network.

USENET introduced the concept of newsgroups, which were discussion groups dedicated to any topic the users wanted to write about. Any user could submit messages to a newsgroup. The messages were available to all the participants. In short, USENET was an electronic bulletin board.

Early USENET newsgroups usually focused on how to operate computers. Soon, however, the focus broadened to include discussions of movies, science fiction, relationships, and countless other subjects. USENET's greatest appeal was that it promoted social interaction among people living far apart who shared common interests.

USENET grew to allow people around the world to connect and have discussions about their shared interests.

# Jeffrey Wilkins's CompuServe

By the early 1980s, online services had sprung up as a popular form of computer communication. These systems were not networks. They were sites that users could connect to and use to send e-mail, post messages, or have online conversations.

The first online service for consumers was CompuServe. Jeffrey Wilkins, a young graduate student at the University of Arizona, founded the company in 1969. At first, it focused on setting up mainframe computers and building data networks for companies. CompuServe's clients accessed the networks using phone lines the company rented from AT&T.

**CompuServe users could access information by choosing topics from a text-based list.**

```
                                    Page 68
CompuServe
        THE COLUMBUS DISPATCH

1 Top News Briefs
2 US/World News
3 Local/Ohio News
4 Political Campaigns
5 Sports
6 Business
7 Opinion/Editorial
8 Leisure/Entertainment


Last menu page. Key digit
or M for previous menu.
```

**Steve Case grew America Online into one of the biggest Internet successes of the 1990s.**

By the late 1970s, Wilkins wanted to tap into the growing market of personal computer owners. With computers and a network already up and running, he sold customers access to his powerful computers, digital storage space, and e-mail and bulletin board services. He also sold downloadable **software**, including games. The service was a tremendous success.

## Steve Case and America Online

In 1985, 27-year-old Steve Case co-founded Quantum Computer Services, another online service company. Six years later, the company's name was changed to America Online (AOL). With Case at the helm, AOL quickly blossomed into the Internet's leading online service provider. By 1994, it had more than one million paying customers. Offering features such as instant messaging, online games, chat rooms, and forums, AOL made online services fun and easy to use. AOL was also more affordable than CompuServe, its main competitor. AOL charged a flat fee of $19.95 per month for unlimited use, while CompuServe charged users for each minute of phone-line access. At its peak in 2002, AOL had almost 27 million subscribers.

AOL used clever marketing strategies such as distributing free computer disks that gave free time on AOL. It even packaged these disks with toys and breakfast cereals. This brought in a steady stream of new customers. America Online was the king of online services.

## Finding What You're Looking For

There were millions of files available on the Internet by the early 1990s, but there was no efficient way to find anything. To solve the dilemma, programmer Mark McCahill and a team of researchers at the University of Minnesota created a protocol called Gopher. Gopher gave information providers the ability to organize files into an arrangement of related topics. Users simply pointed and clicked on the topic they wanted from the menus. Because it was freely distributed on the Internet, Gopher became a popular navigational aid.

The Wide Area Information Server (WAIS) was another tool that made finding things easier. Developed

**AOL gave away millions of CDs offering free time, to build its list of subscribers.**

by the Thinking Machines Corporation in Waltham, Massachusetts, WAIS enabled users to search for files that contained specific words. The names of the files would then be displayed, and the users could select which one they wanted.

Gopher and WAIS helped users find information on the Internet. But the systems could only display text menus, and different files could not be linked together. These concerns were addressed by the creation of the World Wide Web, a development that brought millions of new users to the Internet.

**Tim Berners-Lee recognized that the Internet could become a limitless source of information.**

## Spinning the Web

In the late 1980s, computer scientist Tim Berners-Lee was working at a physics laboratory called CERN, the European Organization for Nuclear Research. Based in Geneva, Switzerland, CERN was home to hundreds of computers brought there by researchers from around the world.

Berners-Lee observed that although personal computers were beginning to use more images, the Internet was limited mainly to text. He wanted to create a system that would allow researchers to create and share all types of media. His early system included text and images. Later versions added audio and video.

Working with fellow computer wizard Robert Cailliau, Berners-Lee created something he called hypertext. It was a way to link files on all computers around the world. By forming such a "world wide web" of information, Berners-Lee planned to create "a pool of human knowledge" that anyone could access. He and other researchers developed a computer language called hypertext markup language (HTML). Using HTML, any type of data—text, image, or movie file—could be called up from the Internet. HTML could also be used to design and create Web sites and their content.

The first version of the World Wide Web began operating at CERN in December 1990. It was an immediate hit with CERN researchers. Several months later, CERN began distributing the Web software over the Internet. The Web, like the invention of printing and television, would soon become one of the most important achievements in the history of human communication.

## A FIRSTHAND LOOK AT
## THE WORLD WIDE WEB

On August 6, 1991, World Wide Web creator Tim Berners-Lee posted a brief summary of the project on the alt.hypertext newsgroup. In his note, he explained how to use the Web browser and told readers to visit his first public Web page. See page 60 for a link to view the original post online.

## Web Browsers

A Web browser is an application that allows a user to access, retrieve, and view information on the Internet. Browsers get people into the Web. One of the first browsers was developed in 1993 by a team led by Marc Andreessen at the University of Illinois. The system was named Mosaic. It was the first to display color images as part of a Web page. Words and pictures were linked, meaning that users could move to other pages with a simple click of the mouse. Mosaic was designed to work on most personal computers. It was distributed free of charge on the Internet

**Marc Andreessen's Netscape Navigator was one of the most popular Web browsers of the 1990s.**

and was instrumental in popularizing the Web.

Andreessen founded the company Netscape with his partner, Jim Clark. In 1994, they launched the Netscape Navigator browser. It was faster and easier to use than Mosaic. Within one year, it became the most widely used Web browser.

The browser war heated up when computer software

giant Microsoft launched its Internet Explorer browser in 1995. A bitter rivalry soon developed between Netscape and Microsoft as Internet Explorer began to draw Navigator's users away from Netscape. Between 2002 and 2003, 95 percent of Web surfers used Internet Explorer. In 2002, Netscape sued Microsoft, claiming that the computer software giant was trying to destroy its business. The case was settled the next year, with Microsoft agreeing to pay Netscape's owners $750 million in exchange for jointly developing new computer software.

**Mozilla's free Firefox browser has become a popular choice for many Internet users in recent years.**

Some of today's most popular browsers are Firefox, Safari, and Chrome. Internet Explorer also remains a favorite with many Internet users.

## The Search Continues

Once a browser gets users into the Web, the users still need a tool to help them find exactly what they want. The tool that helps them locate what they're looking for is called a search engine. Search engines are programs that search for Web sites based on keywords that the user types in. The search engine then sorts through millions of pages in its **database** to locate the information the user is looking for. Within seconds, a list of matches to keywords appears.

Launched in 1994, Yahoo was the first successful commercial search engine. Yahoo was created by Jerry Yang and David Filo, who were doctoral students at Stanford University. It remains a widely used search engine. One of the most popular search engines today is Google. Google started as a research project in 1996 by Stanford University doctoral students Larry Page and Sergey Brin. They chose the name Google because it is an intentional misspelling of the word *googol*, a term for the number one followed by 100 zeros. Page and Brin wanted users to know that Google would organize a huge amount of information.

# A VIEW FROM ABROAD

In 2012, the government of Belarus, in eastern Europe, passed a law to limit access to foreign Web sites. Owners of Internet clubs and coffee shops are required to report users who visit foreign Web sites. They will be fined if they fail to do so. People who break the law can be fined up to $125. This is roughly half the average annual salary in Belarus. Labeled an "outpost of tyranny" by the U.S. government in 2005, Belarus has a long history of censorship and opposition to political freedom.

Today, there are hundreds of search engines specializing in specific areas of interest. Search engines can find Web sites for news, places to shop, audio and video files, government information, travel information, and much more.

# CHAPTER 4

# THE WORLD WIDE WEB TODAY

Thanks to places such as Internet cafés and public libraries, even people who do not own computers can access the World Wide Web.

THE ASTONISHING SUCCESS OF the World Wide Web surprised everyone, including the many dedicated pioneers who developed its amazing technologies. With each passing year, people flock to use the Web in incredible numbers. In 2012, there were roughly 3.2 billion e-mail accounts worldwide. Worldwide Internet usage surged to 2.1 billion people. There were more than 555 million Web sites, with 300 million of them created in 2011 alone.

**Facebook is one of the Web's most visited sites.**

The growth of the Web seems limitless. Every day, users around the globe add new content and develop new Web tools. Many of their innovations have changed the way we live.

## Facebook: The King of Social Networking

More than 900 million people worldwide are active users of Facebook.com, the social networking service that changed communications on the Web. Facebook was founded by Harvard University student Mark Zuckerberg and fellow students Andrew McCollum, Chris Hughes, Eduardo Saverin, and Dustin Moskovitz. The site was launched in February 2004.

Membership in the Web site was originally limited to Harvard students but was soon expanded to other colleges. It then opened to high school students. By 2006, anyone at least 13 years old with an e-mail address could join. Zuckerberg

**SPOTLIGHT ON**

### Mark Zuckerberg

Facebook co-founder Mark Zuckerberg was born in Dobbs Ferry, New York, on May 14, 1984. He developed an interest in computers at age 12 and created an instant messaging program he named Zucknet. In high school, he created a program very similar to the popular online music service Pandora. In 2002, he entered Harvard University, where he began work with his friends on a social networking site. The students ran the site, called The Facebook, out of a dorm room until 2004. Zuckerberg left school to focus on running Facebook full-time. Within months, the site boasted more than one million users.

developed the network so that users could create a personal profile and add other users as their friends. Users can exchange messages and post pictures or videos.

## A VIEW FROM ABROAD

As of 2012, the government of China, the world's most populated nation, does not allow its citizens to access Facebook. In 2007, users in China could access the site, although the connection was never very reliable. In 2009, worldwide users began posting criticisms of China's government on Facebook during a series of riots in the country. In response, the Chinese government blocked the site. Chinese authorities block roughly 2,600 popular Web sites, including Google, YouTube, Twitter, and Wikipedia, the user-contributed online encyclopedia.

Today, thousands of companies and organizations use Facebook as a way to sell their products and services. Politicians have also jumped on the Facebook bandwagon. During the 2008 U.S. presidential elections, candidate Barack Obama's campaign created a Facebook page that attracted more than 2.2 million viewers. These viewers received daily updates from the campaign. Politicians have also found Facebook to be an effective fund-raising tool.

## YouTube: The World's Number One Video-Sharing Service

YouTube.com was created by Chad Hurley, Steve Chen, and Jawed Karim. The three men were co-workers at PayPal, a company that allows people to easily transfer money over the Internet. According to one version of the story, the idea for the site came after Hurley and Chen had problems sharing videos they had taken at a party.

The site was officially launched in December 2005. It was an instant hit. By mid-2006, more than 65,000 new videos were being uploaded by users every day. In 2011, around one trillion videos were viewed on YouTube. That is 140 views per every person in the world. In 2006, YouTube was purchased by Google.

**Internet users can visit YouTube to watch music videos, news reports, TV shows, and much more.**

# A FIRSTHAND LOOK AT

## AN INTERVIEW WITH JEFF BEZOS

Amazon's Kindle e-reader has been one of its most successful products in recent years. Jeff Bezos believes that it will be an important part of the company's future. See page 60 for a link to watch Bezos discuss the Kindle in an interview with Charlie Rose.

## Amazon: The World's Marketplace

Amazon.com was founded by Jeff Bezos in 1994 as an online bookstore. He chose the name Amazon as a reference to the Amazon River, the world's largest river by volume. He wanted his company to have an exotic

**Amazon ships packages to millions of customers every day.**

**Jeff Bezos started Amazon as an online bookstore, but soon grew the company into a one-stop shop for just about anything its customers need.**

name and be huge, like the Amazon. Bezos got his wish. Amazon became the world's largest online retailer.

Today, Amazon sells countless different types of products, such as books, DVDs, clothing, musical instruments, and groceries. In 2007, Amazon began selling Kindle, an electronic book (e-book) reader that downloads digital book content over the Internet. By 2011, Amazon's library of downloadable books numbered almost 900,000.

Bezos came up with the idea for Amazon while driving from New York to Seattle. He wrote up his business plans during the trip and set up the company in his garage upon his return to Seattle.

**Marshall Brain writes about a wide variety of topics for his HowStuffWorks Web site.**

## How Stuff Works

In 1998, computer science professor Marshall Brain got the idea to start a Web site that described how things work. Brain's goal was to explain hard-to-understand concepts in easy-to-understand terms. He achieved this using articles, photos, charts and diagrams, and clever videos and cartoons. The site later added blogs, quizzes, and games to entertain and educate its users.

Users simply type in the subject they want to learn about. They are then directed to pages offering in-depth explanations, tips, and advice. The site covers thousands of topics in subject areas such as electronics, entertainment, and money.

# Pioneers Who Changed the World

The Web has changed the way people communicate, do business, and learn new things. It lets users share news, photos, and music with family and friends. It can teach users almost anything they want to learn, and it can be used almost anywhere—at home, at school, or at work. It entertains users and tells them what's going on in their neighborhoods and around the world. It allows people to learn about and buy products and services that make their lives easier. Web inventors have helped create a new world, and the sky's the limit.

**E-mail and other Internet services have become a necessary part of the way most businesses operate.**

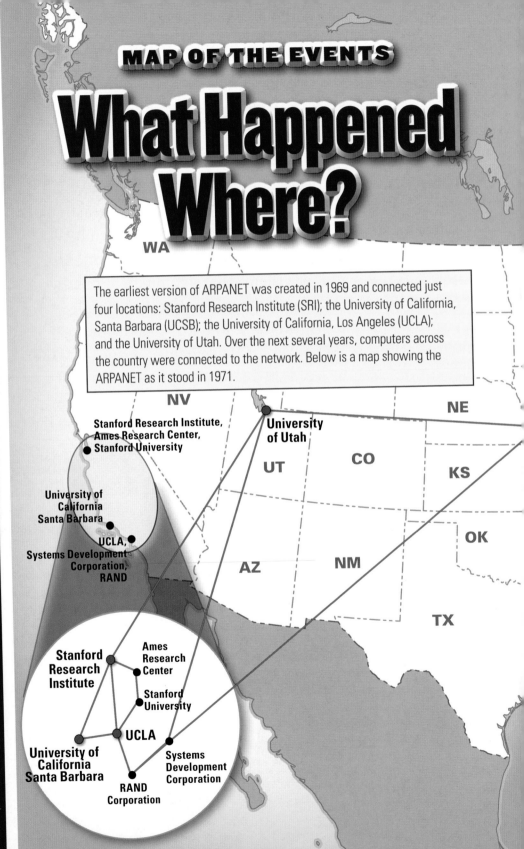

# MAP OF THE EVENTS

# What Happened Where?

WA

The earliest version of ARPANET was created in 1969 and connected just four locations: Stanford Research Institute (SRI); the University of California, Santa Barbara (UCSB); the University of California, Los Angeles (UCLA); and the University of Utah. Over the next several years, computers across the country were connected to the network. Below is a map showing the ARPANET as it stood in 1971.

NV

NE

Stanford Research Institute,
Ames Research Center,
Stanford University

University
of Utah

UT

CO

KS

University of
California
Santa Barbara

UCLA,
Systems Development
Corporation,
RAND

OK

AZ

NM

TX

Stanford
Research
Institute

Ames
Research
Center

Stanford
University

UCLA

University of
California
Santa Barbara

Systems
Development
Corporation

RAND
Corporation

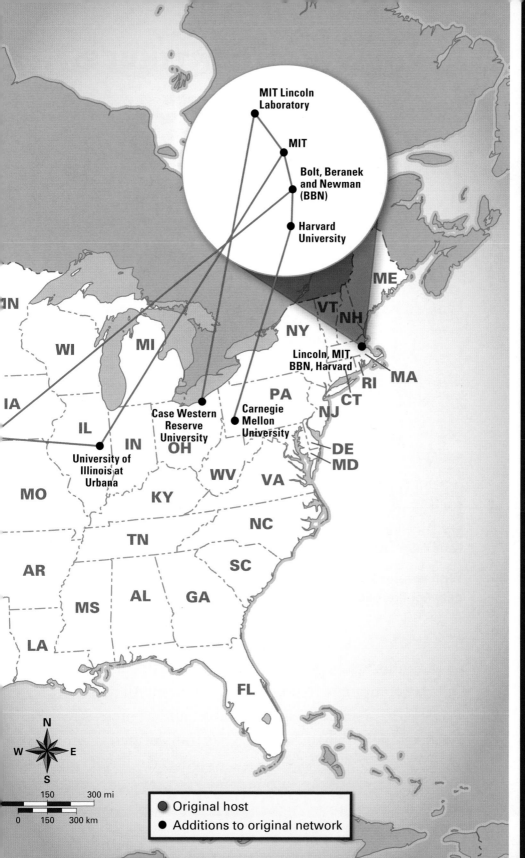

MIT Lincoln
Laboratory

MIT

Bolt, Beranek
and Newman
(BBN)

Harvard
University

ME

VT

NH

NY

Lincoln, MIT,
BBN, Harvard

RI

MA

CT

PA

NJ

Case Western
Reserve
University

Carnegie
Mellon
University

OH

DE

MD

IN

University of
Illinois at
Urbana

WV

VA

MO

KY

NC

TN

AR

SC

MS

AL

GA

LA

FL

IN

WI

MI

IA

IL

N

W          E

S

150        300 mi

0    150    300 km

● Original host
● Additions to original network

# A New Era

**With wireless Internet, computer users no longer need to connect their computers to phone lines or cables.**

The World Wide Web is everywhere. Thanks to recent innovations, users don't even need telephone lines or full-size computers to tap into the Internet. All that is needed is a smartphone or a tablet and a wireless connection. Mobile technology has transformed

**IN 2011, SMARTPHONE SALES PASSED**

traditional telephones into portable, personal multimedia devices. Their development has broadened the reach of the Web and increased the number of Internet users throughout the world.

As the 21st century progresses, new names and faces will change the World Wide Web. What will their next big developments be? More social networking? Faster transmission of information? More wireless networks? Internet access in more devices and products? Only time will tell. If it can be imagined, it just might happen.

**Today's students learn how to use computers when they are very young.**

# INFLUENTIAL INDIVIDUALS

Leonard Kleinrock

**J. C. R. Licklider** (1915–1990) was a computer scientist whose vision of a "Galactic Network" of worldwide interconnected computers was the basis for the modern Internet. From 1962 to 1964, he served as IPTO's first head.

**Wesley Clark** (1927– ) was a computer scientist at Washington University in St. Louis when he suggested that minicomputers be used in the ARPANET's design to handle packet-switching operations.

**Leonard Kleinrock** (1934– ) was a computer science professor at UCLA whose work contributed to the theory of packet switching and the development of the ARPANET.

**Lawrence Roberts** (1937– ) was the program director and, later, director of IPTO and a major contributor to the development of packet switching.

**Robert Kahn** (1938– ) was an ARPA computer manager and director of IPTO whose work with Vinton Cerf on TCP/IP technology helped create the Internet.

**Ray Tomlinson** (1941– ) is a computer programmer who created the first system to send e-mail between different host computers on the ARPANET.

**Vinton Cerf** (1943– ) was a DARPA program manager whose development of TCP/IP technology led to the birth of the Internet.

**Tim Berners-Lee** (1955– ) is a British computer scientist whose development of HTML technology led to the invention of the World Wide Web.

**Mark McCahill** (1956– ) was the head developer of Gopher, the first simple, efficient tool to find information on the Internet.

Vinton Cerf

**Steve Case** (1958– ) is the co-founder of America Online (AOL), the company that pioneered the concept of social interaction on the Internet with features such as chat rooms, instant messaging, and forums.

**Jeff Bezos** (1964– ) is the founder of Amazon .com, the world's largest online retailer. Amazon has grown from selling only books to selling countless different types of products.

Jeff Bezos

**Mark Zuckerberg** (1984– ) is one of the co-founders of Facebook, the world's most popular social networking site.

# TIMELINE

## 1957

The Soviet Union launches and orbits the *Sputnik 1* Earth satellite.

## 1958

The U.S. Department of Defense creates the Advanced Research Projects Agency (ARPA).

## 1962

J. C. R. Licklider joins ARPA as director of its Information Processing Techniques Office.

## 1987

The National Science Foundation takes over operations of DARPANET.

## 1990

DARPANET is decommissioned.

## 1991

The World Wide Web, invented by Tim Berners-Lee, is launched; Mark P. McCahill and a team of researchers create Gopher.

## 1994

The first search engines appear.

## 1969

ARPANET is created; the first network computer message is sent between UCLA and the Stanford Research Institute.

## 1971

Ray Tomlinson sends the first e-mail.

## 1977

The first Internet demonstration occurs, showing that interconnecting different network types is possible.

## 1996

Netscape and Microsoft engage in the Web's first browser war; Google begins as a research project by college students Larry Page and Sergey Brin.

## 2004

Facebook, founded by Mark Zuckerberg and several fellow students, is launched.

## 2005

YouTube is launched.

# LIVING HISTORY

Primary sources provide firsthand evidence about a topic. Witnesses to a historical event create primary sources. They include autobiographies, newspaper reports of the time, oral histories, photographs, and memoirs. A secondary source analyzes primary sources, and is one step or more removed from the event. Secondary sources include textbooks, encyclopedias, and commentaries. To view the following primary and secondary sources, go to www.factsfornow.scholastic.com. Enter the keywords **Internet Inventors** and look for the Living History logo ➤.

➤ **An Accurate Prediction** In 1982, the *New York Times* reported the National Science Foundation's prediction that electronic information technology would change our world. Go online to read the article.

➤ **An Interview with Jeff Bezos** Watch as journalist Charlie Rose speaks with Amazon.com founder Jeff Bezos about the Amazon Kindle e-reader.

➤ *Sputnik I* Go online to read a *New York Times* account of the launch and orbit of *Sputnik 1*.

➤ **The World Wide Web** Go online to view Tim Berners-Lee's 1991 newsgroup posting that encouraged researchers to try his new Web technology.

# RESOURCES

## Books

Duffield, Katy. *Chad Hurley, Steve Chen, Jawed Karim: YouTube Creators*. Farmington Hills, MI: KidHaven Press, 2008.

Gilbert, Sara. *The Story of Google*. Mankato, MN: Creative Education, 2009.

McPherson, Stephanie Sammartino. *Tim Berners-Lee: Inventor of the World Wide Web*. Minneapolis: Twenty-First Century Books, 2010.

Visit this Scholastic Web site for more information on Internet inventors:
**www.factsfornow.scholastic.com**
Enter the keywords **Internet Inventors**

# GLOSSARY

**broadcasting** (BRAWD-kas-ting) sending out radio or television signals

**database** (DAY-tuh-base) a set of related information that is organized and stored in a computer, as in a database of addresses

**digitized** (DIJ-i-tized) converted or changed data or graphic images to digital form usable by a computer

**hardware** (HAHRD-wair) computer equipment

**Internet** (IN-tur-net) the electronic network that allows millions of computers around the world to connect together

**keywords** (KEE-wurdz) words that can be used to find a particular book, Web site, or computer file

**modems** (MOH-duhmz) electronic devices that allow computers to exchange data, especially over a telephone line

**network** (NET-wurk) a group of connected computers or communications equipment

**protocol** (PROH-tuh-kawl) a set of rules about how data is moved between computers over a network so that no information is lost

**software** (SAWFT-wair) computer programs

# INDEX

Page numbers in *italics* indicate illustrations.

# ABOUT THE AUTHOR

**Nel Yomtov** is an award-winning author of nonfiction books and graphic novels for young readers. He lives in the New York City area.

mL                          6-13